OUR SOLAR SYSTEM
THE MOON
EARTH'S SATELLITE

by Mari Schuh

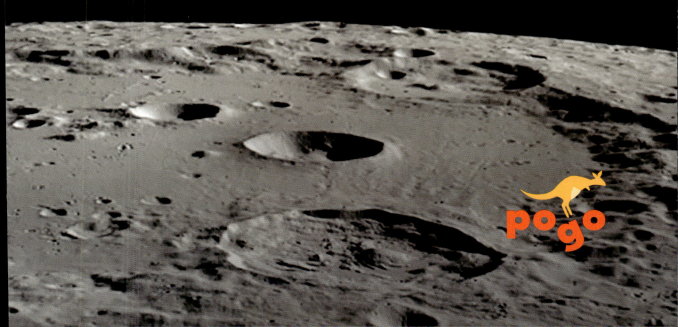

Ideas for Parents and Teachers

Pogo Books let children practice reading informational text while introducing them to nonfiction features such as headings, labels, sidebars, maps, and diagrams, as well as a table of contents, glossary, and index.

Carefully leveled text with a strong photo match offers early fluent readers the support they need to succeed.

Before Reading

- "Walk" through the book and point out the various nonfiction features. Ask the student what purpose each feature serves.
- Look at the glossary together. Read and discuss the words.

Read the Book

- Have the child read the book independently.
- Invite him or her to list questions that arise from reading.

After Reading

- Discuss the child's questions. Talk about how he or she might find answers to those questions.
- Prompt the child to think more. Ask: The Moon's surface is covered with craters. How did these craters form?

Pogo Books are published by Jump!
5357 Penn Avenue South
Minneapolis, MN 55419
www.jumplibrary.com

Copyright © 2023 Jump!
International copyright reserved in all countries.
No part of this book may be reproduced in any form without written permission from the publisher.

Library of Congress Cataloging-in-Publication Data is available at www.loc.gov or upon request from the publisher.

ISBN: 979-8-88524-358-2 (hardcover)
ISBN: 979-8-88524-359-9 (paperback)
ISBN: 979-8-88524-360-5 (ebook)

Editor: Jenna Gleisner
Designer: Emma Bersie

Photo Credits: Slatan/Shutterstock, cover (background); astronightskies/Shutterstock, cover (Moon); muratart/Shutterstock, 1; Narupon Nimpaiboon/Shutterstock, 3; Kriengsuk Prasroetsung, 4; Doug Lemke/Shutterstock, 5; Diczie Quiel Sarino/Shutterstock, 6–7; Peter Burnett/iStock, 8–9; OceanicWanderer/Shutterstock, 10; Siberian Art/Shutterstock, 11; Castleski/Shutterstock, 12–13 (phases); Ivan Popovych/Shutterstock, 12–13 (background); buradaki/Shutterstock, 14–15; NASA/JPL, 16–17; Stanislaw Tokarski/Alamy, 18; NASA, 19, 20–21; NASA Goddard, 23 (left), 23 (right).

Printed in the United States of America at Corporate Graphics in North Mankato, Minnesota.

For Paige

TABLE OF CONTENTS

CHAPTER 1
Earth's Satellite...................................4

CHAPTER 2
All About the Moon..........................10

CHAPTER 3
Amazing Discoveries........................18

ACTIVITIES & TOOLS
Try This!..22
Glossary..23
Index...24
To Learn More...................................24

CHAPTER 1
EARTH'S SATELLITE

The Moon is the biggest and brightest object in Earth's night sky.

We can also see the Moon during the day. It is about 238,855 miles (384,400 kilometers) away from Earth.

CHAPTER 1   5

The Moon orbits, or travels in circles around, Earth. It is Earth's only natural **satellite**.

CHAPTER 1

TAKE A LOOK!

The Moon is part of our **solar system**. It is much smaller than Earth. Take a look!

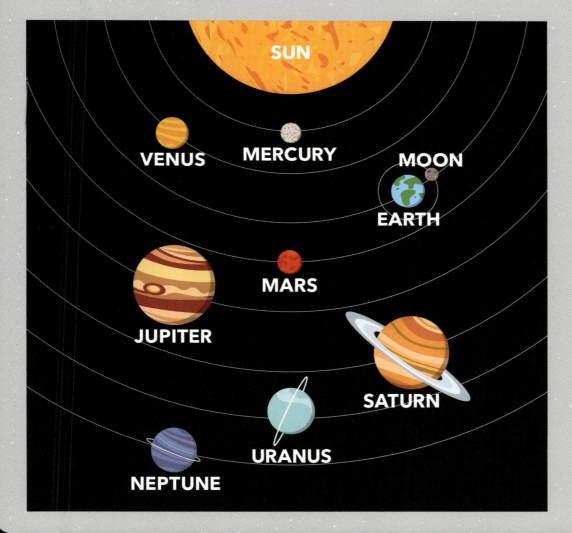

All objects have **gravity**. The Moon's gravity pulls on Earth. This pull moves Earth's oceans. It creates **tides**.

DID YOU KNOW?

An object's gravity depends on its size, **mass**, and **density**. Gravity on the Moon is not as strong as it is on Earth. Let's say you weigh 100 pounds (45 kilograms). On the Moon, you would weigh only 16 pounds (7.3 kg)!

CHAPTER 1

CHAPTER 2
ALL ABOUT THE MOON

The Moon spins, just like the **planets**. One full spin around is one day. The Moon spins slowly. One day on the Moon is about 27 Earth days.

The Moon's orbit around Earth also takes about 27 Earth days. So the Moon spins only once every time it travels around Earth. This means the same side of the Moon always faces Earth. The side we see is called the near side. The side we can't see is called the far side.

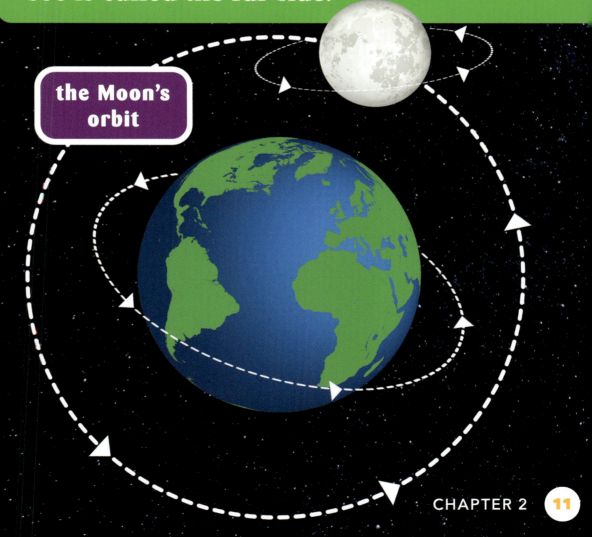

the Moon's orbit

CHAPTER 2

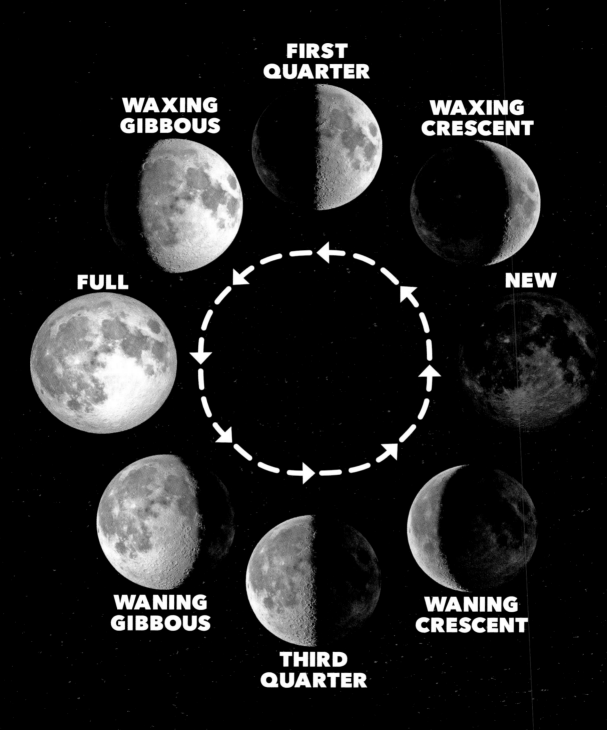

As the Moon orbits, sunlight hits different areas. It makes the Moon look like different shapes. These are **phases**. We see them from Earth.

A full moon looks like a complete circle. It is bright. Why? During a full moon, all of the Moon's near side **reflects** light from the Sun.

DID YOU KNOW?

As the Moon orbits, sometimes Earth comes between it and the Sun. Earth blocks the sunlight. It casts a shadow on the Moon. This is called a lunar eclipse.

The Moon has a very thin **atmosphere**. It has no wind and no weather. During the day, its surface is hot. Temperatures can be 225 degrees Fahrenheit (107 degrees Celsius). At night, temperatures drop. It can be −243 degrees Fahrenheit (−153 degrees Celsius).

CHAPTER 2 15

The Moon's thin atmosphere cannot stop **meteorites**. They crash into the Moon. They leave **craters** and damage the Moon's surface.

crater

TAKE A LOOK!

The Moon is mostly made of rock. What are its layers? Take a look!

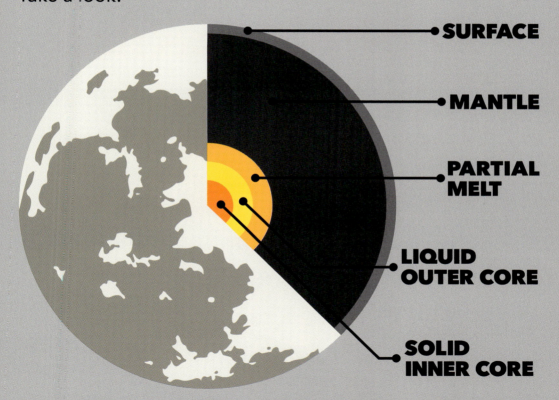

CHAPTER 3

AMAZING DISCOVERIES

In 1959, the space **probe** *Luna 3* visited the Moon. It took the first photos of the Moon's far side. Since then, more than 100 **spacecraft** have explored the Moon.

Luna 3

In 1969, U.S. **astronauts** went to the Moon. They were the first people to walk on it.

CHAPTER 3   19

The astronauts left footprints in the Moon's dust. The footprints are still there. Why? The Moon has no wind to blow them away.

The astronauts collected rocks and soil. Scientists are still studying them today. What more would you like to discover about the Moon?

DID YOU KNOW?

In 2020, scientists discovered water on a sunny area of the Moon. Scientists have not found signs of life on the Moon. But someday, people might be able to live on it!

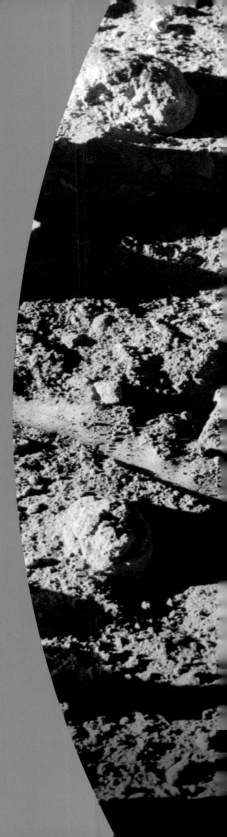

CHAPTER 3

ACTIVITIES & TOOLS

TRY THIS!

MOON PHASE COOKIES

The Moon's phases make it look different when we look at it from Earth. Create the Moon's different phases in this fun activity!

What You Need:
- sandwich cookies with frosting inside
- plate
- butter knife or fork

❶ Carefully twist the cookie to separate the pieces. Does all the frosting stick to one side? If so, this cookie looks like a full moon.

❷ Use a butter knife or fork to scrape the frosting off just the left half of the cookie. Now the cookie looks like the Moon's first quarter phase.

❸ Next, scrape the rest of the frosting off so that there is no more frosting left on the cookie. Now the cookie looks like a new moon.

❹ If you have more cookies, scrape the frosting into other shapes to create different phases of the Moon. Then, enjoy the cookies!

GLOSSARY

astronauts: People trained to travel and work in space.

atmosphere: The mixture of gases that surrounds a planet.

craters: Large holes in the ground that are made when pieces of rock or metal in space crash into a planet or moon.

density: The measure of how heavy or light an object is for its size. Density is measured by dividing an object's mass by its volume.

gravity: The force that pulls things toward the center of a planet or body and keeps them from floating away.

mass: The amount of physical matter an object has.

meteorites: Pieces of rock or metal in space that hit a planet or moon.

phases: Stages of the Moon's changes in shape as it appears from Earth.

planets: Large bodies that orbit, or travel in circles around, the Sun.

probe: A tool or device used to explore or examine something.

reflects: Throws back light, heat, or sound from a surface.

satellite: A moon or other object that orbits a larger object in space.

solar system: The Sun, together with its orbiting bodies, such as the planets, their moons, and asteroids, comets, and meteors.

spacecraft: Vehicles that travel in space.

tides: The constant changes in sea level that are caused by the pull of the Moon and the Sun on Earth.

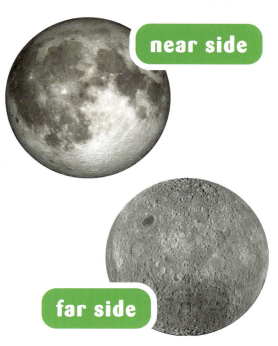

near side

far side

ACTIVITIES & TOOLS 23

INDEX

astronauts 19, 20
atmosphere 14, 16
craters 16
day 5, 10, 11, 14
dust 20
Earth 4, 5, 6, 7, 8, 10, 11, 13
far side 11, 18
full moon 13
gravity 8
layers 17
Luna 3 18
lunar eclipse 13

meteorites 16
near side 11, 13
orbits 6, 11, 13
phases 13
reflects 13
satellite 6
solar system 7
Sun 7, 13
surface 14, 16, 17
temperatures 14
tides 8
water 20

TO LEARN MORE

Finding more information is as easy as 1, 2, 3.

❶ Go to www.factsurfer.com
❷ Enter "Moon" into the search box.
❸ Choose your book to see a list of websites.

ACTIVITIES & TOOLS